War Without Heroes

David Douglas Duncan

Harper & Row
Publishers

New York and Evanston

War
Without
Heroes

Photography – text – design – production:
David Douglas Duncan

Printing; sheet-fed gravure:
Enschedé en Zonen, Haarlem, the Netherlands

Binding:
Van Rijmenam N.V., the Hague

FIRST EDITION
LIBRARY OF CONGRESS CATALOG CARD NUMBER: 70-123926

Page 251: *The Bible, Psalm 86 : 1-4.*

Books by D.D.D.
War Without Heroes
Self-Portrait: U.S.A.
I Protest!
Yankee Nomad
Picasso's Picassos
The Kremlin
The Private World of Pablo Picasso
This Is War!

Foreword

There is neither climax nor conclusion to this book. It is simply an effort to show what a man endures when his country decides to go to war, with or without his personal agreement on the righteousness of the cause.

I wanted to show what war does to a man. I wanted to show the comradeship that binds men together when they are fighting a common peril. I wanted to show the way men live, and die, when they know death is among them, and yet they still find the strength to crawl forward armed only with bayonets to stop the advance of men they have never seen, with whom they have no immediate quarrel, men who will kill them on sight if given first chance. I wanted to show the agony, the suffering, the terrible confusion, the heroism which is everyday currency among those men who actually pull the triggers of rifles aimed at other men known as "the enemy." I wanted to tell a story of war, as war has always been for men. Only their weapons, the terrain, the causes have changed.

I wrote the above words nineteen years ago as an explanation for *This Is War!*, a book based on the "police action" in Korea. Now, once again, the same lines seem appropriate for this new book about Americans fighting in Asia where, once again, our troops have been ordered into combat in another undeclared war.

Nearly every man in this book is a Marine. It is no accident. I was with them during World War II, and in Korea. I rejoined them in Viet-Nam in 1967 and 1968 for three combat operations along the Demilitarized Zone, where I took the photographs in this book. But these pages could just as well have been filled with pictures of soldiers or paratroopers or medevac pilots, or any number of other Americans in uniform in "Nam," whose lives there were much the same.

My photographs reveal only what these men did, perhaps something of what they felt and probably very little of what they thought. Not a man, to my knowledge, was decorated for an act of valor performed during any action recorded here. In their own eyes, they were participating in everyday events while serving in a foreign land where their country was at war...a war without heroes.

After years of fighting in Viet-Nam and for the first time in our history, we have not hailed the birth of a single military legend: no MacArthurs, Eisenhowers or Doolittles; no Audie Murphys, Colin Kellys or Pappy Boyingtons; no Sergeant Yorks, Black Jack Pershings or Eddie Rickenbackers; no Davy Crocketts; no Custers; no Lees, Grants or Shermans; no George Washingtons—*nobody*. In fact, we haven't even had a special U.S. Treasury Bond drive for the wounded. All we have had are the exhortations of four Presidents—and the Pentagon—enshrining the virtues and necessities of an alliance with coup-oriented Saigon in order to promote and protect an extension of our own democratic way of life in Southeast Asia. So the Marines and their fellow Army troopers were shipped out, with the Leathernecks being given the northernmost region fringing the DMZ.

This war has now become the longest in our nation's history. It is a war that has taken more lives than those lost in Korea, a war that shattered the power of, and then deposed, a President of the United States. And, of significance beyond the vision of any man today to judge, it is a war that has fractured the substructure of our society to a depth which will require the efforts of yet unborn generations to heal. Even then nothing will be the same. For one conclusion already seems clear: our involvement in Viet-Nam has emerged as the greatest American tragedy since the Civil War.

Today, many lives and years later, there still has been no Congressional declaration of war against "the enemy." And yet, today, more than three million American men have borne arms and participated in making war against another nation—remote, obscure and isolated from them in every way: military men invested for political ends, although very few Americans had ever seen a Vietnamese—South or North—until they were sent to fight in the jungles of Southeast Asia.

These photographs have now been reassembled with affection for those men who so often shared all they possessed with a stranger, and as a tribute to their code of values—courage; generosity in its most pure form; simplicity of language where words had no hidden meanings; responsibility to their comrades, convictions and pride.

This book is also my effort toward a portrait of that man alone in the trenches—an image which he created of himself during endless days and nights on the battlefield.

New York City   D.D.D.
Earth Day
22 April, 1970

Courage is a moral quality; it is not a chance gift of nature like an aptitude for games. It is a cold choice between two alternatives, the fixed resolve not to quit; an act of renunciation which must be made not once but many times by the power of the will.

Courage is will power.

Lord Moran
The Anatomy of Courage

I DEDICATE THIS BOOK
TO THE
"TOMORROW"
IN EVERY SOLDIER'S PRAYER

"Here Lies
Pham-Ngoc-Linh
Partisan
3/6 R.I.C.
Died For France
20–6–50"

Hanoi, Indochina,
French Military Cemetery
22 May, 1953

There, too, lay the heart
of the problem.
In the jungled mountains
to the north,
on the frontier of China,
an old man,
Ho Chi Minh,
spoke:
"*We* offer our lives,
and *we* die,
for Viet-Nam!"

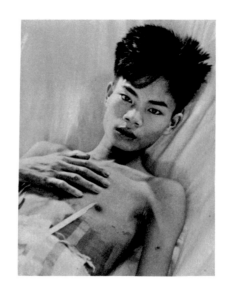

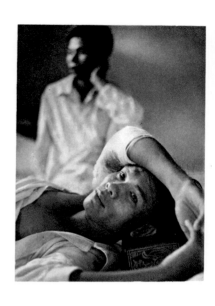

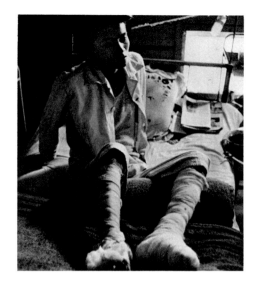

Those Vietnamese-French recruits in
Hanoi looked just the way I felt
the day they sent *us* off to war.
We'd polished rifles and shoes since
dawn; holding ranks—we'd drilled for
three months; proud—the Marine Corps
Hymn gagged in our throats; we were
so sure all eyes were upon us some
later claimed they made it the
whole way looking at the ground.
Then away we went—and friends fell,
yet the pride of that first day
followed them into their graves.

A tragic French failing was that when
a Vietnamese soldier fought and died,
he was buried without honor—
and his family was left alone.

Auvergnats, Bretons, Alsatians, Normans, Parisians—
Laotians, Annamese, Tonkinese, Senegalese, Soudanese—
Moroccans, Mauritanians, Guineans, Algerians—
pilots, cooks, paratroopers, medics—
tankmen, artillerymen, commando Legionnaires—
the wounded and the dead
soldiers of France:
all were there—by the hundreds of thousands.
There would be no more...
not Frenchmen.
It was now nearly over.
They were the tragedy—the cause was bankrupt from the start.

  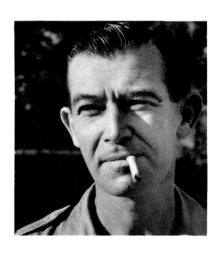 

On 7 May, 1954, the French garrison at Dien Bien Phu—without medical supplies or air cover or ammunition and encircled by the Communist Vietminh, who possessed massed artillery which obliterated any hope of salvation or significant reinforcement—was overrun by the enemy.

In Washington, the White House was occupied by Dwight David Eisenhower, a five-star general of the armies who had led the Western Allies during their "Crusade in Europe" against totalitarian domination. His Secretary of State, John Foster Dulles, was to make "brinkmanship," and its implied threat to aggressors, known throughout the world. In the international waters of the South China Sea, squadrons of U.S. Seventh Fleet aircraft carriers were on patrol. Other squadrons cruised the Pacific and, in carrier time, the nearby Mediterranean and Atlantic. Yet, by May 7, when the ten thousand French soldiers still alive at Dien Bien Phu lifted their hands in surrender to the Communists, only Frenchmen had tried to send relief. America sent a telegram of encouragement. Our carriers stayed on stations in the China Sea, Pacific, Mediterranean and Atlantic, alert to any overt Communist threat.

At the Geneva Cease-Fire Conference of 21 July, 1954 (which the United States had pressed to convene, then refused to support as a fully participating signatory member), a new Premier, Pierre Mendès-France, accepted for France the Articles of Accord whereby a Communist state, "The Democratic Republic of Viet-Nam," came into being. Indochina was cut at the 17th parallel. Ho Chi Minh, one of the oldest and canniest of Asian Communists, became the first President of his "People's Republic"—North Viet-Nam—its capital Hanoi.

Saigon became the capital of South Viet-Nam, the other half of the newly partitioned land; a division accepted by the belligerents in Geneva as a means of separating their warring armies. The military partition of Indochina in 1954 was intended to be only temporary. The political future of the entire country was to be decided by a free, secret, internationally supervised election in July, 1956—which never took place. Each side later accused the other of sabotaging the election. Civil war erupted. The Soviet Union and Communist China supported North Viet-Nam against South Viet-Nam, which quickly became an ever more strife-ridden and demanding ward of the United States—which, in turn, met the Communist threat by escalating its own tactics and commitments until by the mid-1960s Americans were bombing North Viet-Nam, in support of the more than five hundred thousand soldiers sailors, airmen and Marines in South Viet-Nam. For the third time in one generation the United States was fighting in Asia; now—as in Korea—locked in another bitter, undeclared war where everything except lethal gas and the hydrogen bomb would be employed as weapons.

Caught between giants, Indochina soon lay crushed—but not dying—a once-verdant land where the blood of nearly fifty thousand dead Americans has seeped into its jungle floor, there mixing with the blood of seventy-five thousand Frenchmen who fell, and the more than one million Vietnamese killed in the seemingly endless battle for the tragic place which they called home.

8

September

1967
Cua Viet

News Release

Office of Information
United States Military Assistance Command Vietnam
Release number: 262–67   19 September 1967

MACV Communiqué

Operation FORTRESS SENTRY commenced on 17 September with an early morning amphibious-heliborne assault in northern Quang Tri Province. The search-and-destroy operation is being conducted by a 3rd Marines Battalion Landing Team from the U.S. Navy's 7th Fleet Special Landing Force. The area is along the coastal plain just below the DMZ, 10 km (6 miles) northeast of Dong Ha. There have been no significant enemy contacts reported in the operation.

Five lines of copy in a twelve-page press handout—and surely ignored by nearly all the foreign correspondents assigned to Viet-Nam—the communiqué was just a droplet in the flood of words surging from the war. As news, Fortress Sentry produced nothing meriting a headline anywhere. Even those thousand-odd Marines committed to the operation would have agreed. Was it their eleventh—or ninth—such mission since the Special Landing Force began striking from the Gulf of Tonkin, the previous May? Few remembered or kept score, or knew its code name. September 17—D-Day for Fortress Sentry—would probably be remembered by the Marines as being different from other landings only because it ran afoul of the first great autumnal monsoon storm of the year—in no press release.

Twenty-knot winds lifted a midnight sea full against the Marines' amphibious assault ship, the *USS Tripoli*, smashing landing craft and landing timetable alike. Escort tanks and amphibious tractors had been scheduled to race five miles north, under predawn protective darkness, from the estuary of the Cua Viet River to the Demilitarized Zone—straight toward the snouts of enemy artillery hidden in caves just across the frontier. It was noon before the armored task force finally spun around to a clanking halt on the edge of that unmarked, cloudburst-veiled, international no-man's-land, now known everywhere as the DMZ. But the Marines were lucky: enemy artillery fire control was also momentarily thrown off balance by the storm, and out of radio contact with their forward observers stationed among the dunes south of the DMZ. It was to be a reprieve of short duration.

Fortress Sentry was scheduled with the hope of duplicating the success of another sweep ten days earlier through the same dunes, when eighty-seven Soviet-made 122-millimeter rockets were captured—cradled comfortably in their simple sand-scooped launching ramps and aimed at the Marines' forward positions in Cua Viet and Dong Ha, a few miles to the south. No official communiqué had trumpeted the Marines' rocket coup. And even now, not a word suggested that there might be any mission other than search and destroy assigned to Fortress Sentry.

The primary objective of the operation was to overrun and then secure a sandpatch of high ground abutting the DMZ itself—the northernmost position to be staked out on the Tonkin Gulf.

The ultrasecret mission of the Fortress Sentry Marines' strike was to establish what was intended to be the easternmost fire outpost anchoring the optimistically conceived but ill-fated electronic "McNamara Line," soon abandoned, rusting, deep in the DMZ rain forest.

Except for flash storms which turned a gray day into near-night and the operations officers' ornately colored maps into scraps of meaningless paper, and the scrub-foliaged dunes into deadly tractor-miring swamps, the opening twenty-four hours of Fortress Sentry rumbled by with very little to distinguish them from many other hours of many other days, of many months already spent by the same Marines in that far-from-home land to which they had been shipped for combat duty. It was, as described by the major commanding the amtrac assault force, "just an ordinary day."

Was it their eleventh?
—or ninth?—such mission
since they began striking
from the Gulf of Tonkin,
the previous May.
Few remembered,
or kept score.

September 17—D-Day—
would probably be
remembered by the
Marines because it ran
afoul of the first great
autumnal monsoon storm
of the year.

Most of the men
just bent their heads
against the wind and rain,
and waited....

Fortress Sentry's brass was reluctant to cancel the operation even after the monsoon hit. They were gambling on a few knots of wind dropping off when the assault craft were launched—and won. Though late, the last Marine was safely on Red Beach before noon.

By nightfall, the seas were eight feet high and tossing landing craft sideways on the river bank—which was Red Beach—and had turned the Cua Viet estuary into a seething nightmare. But by then the operation could be supported by everything brought ashore with the Marines themselves. Helicopters appeared through the downpour, barely skimming the dunes, keeping the amtracs under observation as much as possible while supplying eyes for naval gunfire support, if needed—which would be soon.

Later, a Saigon press communiqué described the Marines as having "stormed ashore" at Cua Viet to get on Red Beach. Actually, it was a most casual affair, with the troopers probing for shallow bottom while risking as little salt-water damage as possible to their gear.

A couple of Vietnamese net fishermen stoically watched the show standing in tidal pools along the north bank of the Cua Viet River, five miles south of the DMZ and Ben Hai River (dividing South from North Viet-Nam), where enemy gunners in camouflaged caves would have had a turkey shoot had the storm lifted. Instead, twenty inches of rain flooded the beachhead area within twenty-four hours.

Amtracs of Foxtrot Company, 2nd Battalion, 3rd Marines,
roared north from their Cua Viet River beachhead with one tread
in the Tonkin Gulf surf and the other on the sand, hoping to avoid
enemy mines. And as they disappeared, then reappeared, in the
monsoon mists, the Marine-encrusted caravan seemed reminiscent
of those earlier western stagecoaches and the way *they* must have
looked when headed out, at full gallop, through Indian country.

Captain Reginald G. Ponsford III, commanding officer of
Foxtrot Company, 2/3 Marines, led the point assault force to the
DMZ, then veered inland and again to the beach, finally returning
to Cua Viet—a typical search-and-destroy mission for his amtracmen.
Broken-nosed, icy-eyed, shaven head and a heavyweight wrestler's
build—with fading tattoos—Captain Ponsford of El Paso, Texas,
personified all that one might have hoped to find in a Marine officer
to accompany when participating in such a mission.

Earlier, aboard the *USS Tripoli* the night before the landing,
when told of the operation's picture possibilities, he had stood,
shoulders sloping down, hands motionless at his sides, feet braced
slightly apart and seemingly riveted into the ship's deck to hold
him steady against the roll. He just nodded—listening without
the slightest change of expression. It was as though he had
answered: "Well, okay...that's another profession. I have mine."
But he offered the hitchhiking camera a ride atop his amtrac
during the bone-wracking sprint to the DMZ.

Even though Captain Ponsford had hit the same area only ten days earlier—when it was ideal amtrac country—the storm had now changed everything, even grounding the observation helicopters. A second amtrac swung alongside Ponsford's, while he and its commander tried to decide just where the hell they were in that godforsaken bit of sodden wilderness—with General Giap's gunners waiting to welcome them up the beach.

Churning inland across the dunes, Captain Ponsford scouted a
path—often afoot—as he moved his amtracs forward. By this
time the land was disappearing under rapidly rising water
which turned every ravine between the dunes into a river,
and the flatlands into a vast marsh. Amtracs began getting stuck.
There was no swinging around them without facing the immediate
danger of striking mines, known to be sown throughout the area.
Except for the monsoon-bred lakes appearing suddenly from
nowhere, the DMZ could have been mistaken for a North African
desert. And the dunes and sparse foliage and nearly endless
sweep of tank-torn sand would have offered Montgomery and
Rommel familiar challenges, as each fought to ensnare the other.

The land, here, was a bleak quagmire, seemingly waiting to suck the treads right off amphibious tractors—those not already bogged down and dead in flash-flood potholes. For many of the Marines—riflemen, machine gunners and all of the others riding on top of the amtracs with nothing to do but crouch low upon the steel shell and wait for the armored caravan to roll again—for those men each delay was cruel torture. They knew that every nearby sand dune, or wisp of brush, or rain-veiled hillock might easily be *the* place chosen by a Vietcong forward observer to lie motionless for hours beside his radio, waiting to whisper cryptic target coordinates back to those other patient rocket and artillerymen, north of the DMZ.

One delay led to another. There was no sign of close air support
moving in to provide cover, or to keep the enemy gunners back
inside their caves along the Ben Hai River, just beyond the DMZ.
Captain Ponsford became ever more wary and apprehensive.
He stood bareheaded atop his amtrac and warned of the danger
of imminent artillery attack—that each man must be prepared
to take instant protective measures, especially abandoning the
amtracs, which were primary targets. There would be little time!

Even at that moment the shells were coming in....

The first salvo fell around the lead tank—a second salvo then geysered alongside the amtracs. And it began pouring again as the Marines dived for cover in the surrounding dunes. Crewmen of the mired amtrac stayed to free it, to open the way for all of the others to escape to the beach.

Enemy machine gunners farther back along the column brought those men under harassing fire. Someone, in almost innocent outrage, yelled: "Those bastards have an FO in this place!"—as his heels disappeared over a nearby dune... "FO", for "forward observer", and he was good.

The rain added a mood of blurred surrealism to the artillery attack, exaggerating an acute feeling of how slowly everyone moved —even though racing— while dodging around the casual figure of Captain Ponsford, who stood facing the flow of his running Marines, guiding them to shelter.

The stuck amtrac was finally
freed. Its helmetless wildman
marvelous gunner bellowed above
explosions and monsoon wind
at the other driver to cut his
engine, remove towline—roll!

Captain Ponsford, even with his
amtracs moving again, desperately
tried calling for naval shelling
of the enemy gunners, but his
radio was half-dead in the rain.
He was sure the momentary lull
in the attack was exactly that:
the hidden FO was sending new
coordinates to his fire control
officer, or he was himself also
fighting a broken-down radio.
Ponsford's radioman watched his
captain with almost stricken
eyes, unmoving, but adoring,
as though, for that moment,
Captain Reginald Ponsford III
was very nearly his god, in
control of all their destinies.

36

No sooner had the amtrac column begun advancing cautiously,
than artillery air-bursts exploded overhead. Captain Ponsford had
guessed enemy tactics. And, again on the radio, he tried to direct
counterbattery fire, making the best of his rather awkward role
of being the center of the enemy target. His Marines clawed
futilely at the steel roof of their amtrac digging imaginary foxholes,
then lay still, flattened and waiting—everything else was too late.
Direct hits, or detonating land mines, could have incinerated them
had they sought protection inside. Air-bursts caught amtracs farther
back in the column, spraying shrapnel down upon the men.
There were casualties. And, as during the earlier attack, concealed
machine gunners took the pinned-down Marines under fire, sending
everyone diving for battle positions behind ancient Vietnamese
tombstones and graveyard walls, scattered among the surrounding
dunes. After a naked fifteen minutes of air-bursts, rockets and light
machine-gun fire, two helicopters finally reached the column,
darting under the storm clouds. Muffled but massive explosions
rumbled down from the north—naval gunfire. The Marines
remounted their amtracs to move away from that desolate place.

Later, it was discovered that the monsoon storm had even left its
marks upon the negatives taken that day. Fearsome streaks ripped
through every picture made when the amtracs were being showered by
air-bursts: apparently the column was at the epicenter of the tempest.
Static electricity crackled everywhere, especially inside the camera.

A shuddering blast carried over the engines—another amtrac farther down the line had struck a mine: the whole column was again immobilized until the lead tractor could work its way around the flaming wreck, while demolition experts cleared the path, wary of stepping upon other mines.

The amtrac driver was lucky: first-degree burns and one broken leg.
Still, he was the first man off and vaulting into the sand dunes
after the explosion. Four other amtracs struck mines during that
long, twenty-four-hour, violence-filled day. More than forty Marines
were wounded in the blasts and, in some cases, fires when fuel
tanks exploded. Generally, it was the drivers who were worst injured,
the other men being semiprotected by sandbags on the tractor decks—
and the fact that everyone but the driver and copilot rode on the roof.

The sheer desolation of the dunelands in that coastal area south
of the DMZ was appalling: only gray fiddler crabs scurried across
the sand, while an occasional, thin, low-flying wedge of ducks veered
sharply away from the Marines atop their lurching vehicles. A single
pheasant boomed aloft, then beat its way north, toward the DMZ.
One bent-over farm couple was sighted working a pathetic, stamp-
sized rice paddy in the far distance. Few Marines troubled even
to look at them. It was a place filled with Nature's sad song of
hopeless earth and brackish water, where man was a stranger—alone.

The Marines had eyes only for food—they had seen other amtracs
burning many times before.

An old hand from the Korean War, Major Wendall Beard, shepherded the entire task force. He lived comfortably atop his monstrous amtrac, where he also held court much like an Arab sheikh— regally ignoring the monsoon cloudbursts raging across his local desert domain.
The Major had left the Marines for one season to play professional football as "Moose" Beard of the Washington Redskins, but then he returned home to the drab-green uniform after "some really big guys worked on me—taking out two ribs." Major Beard stood six feet four and weighed about two hundred and thirty pounds—totally unflappable, confident of his Marines, a natural commander.

When Colonel Ronald Mason, operations officer of the landing force from the *Tripoli*, helicoptered in to check on the column, he arrived without helmet or battle gear—evidence of another world only minutes away. Major Beard welcomed him with casual surprise, especially after learning of headquarters' concern that enemy fire might make him abandon his mission. Moose Beard grunted, with a contemptuous thumb poked back over one shoulder toward the nearby DMZ...
followed by a massive finger rammed at his beloved amtrac:
"Those clowns? Send hot chow. We're staying here!"

"Who's worried...

...it's just an ordinary day."

After his visitor had flown away, and after his Marines had dug tight
necklaces of already swamped foxholes around their amtracs to protect
them through the night—while the monsoon pummeled his men
and their weapons and every other living thing and all of the ghastly
land around them with cloudburst that followed cloudburst—
Major Wendall Beard sat atop his amtrac with his drenched cigarette,
fully aware of the price paid for *that* day—that ordinary day—by his
men now lying motionless in hospital beds back aboard the *Tripoli*.

One young Marine rifleman, hit by an artillery air-burst, was placed
on the ship's operating table within thirty minutes after being wounded.
Had the delay been longer, he would not have survived. His chances
of recovery were only fifty-fifty at the end of the second day.
Shrapnel had entered his lower back, left of the spine, but there
was no apparent paralysis. Two lumbar vertebrae were destroyed.
His left kidney was fragmented, removed. His spleen was fragmented,
removed; as were sections of both his large and small intestines.
Shrapnel had punctured his chest diaphragm, but it was repaired.
Hospital orderlies would be standing watch twenty-four hours a day
over the Marine until he recovered...or until he died.

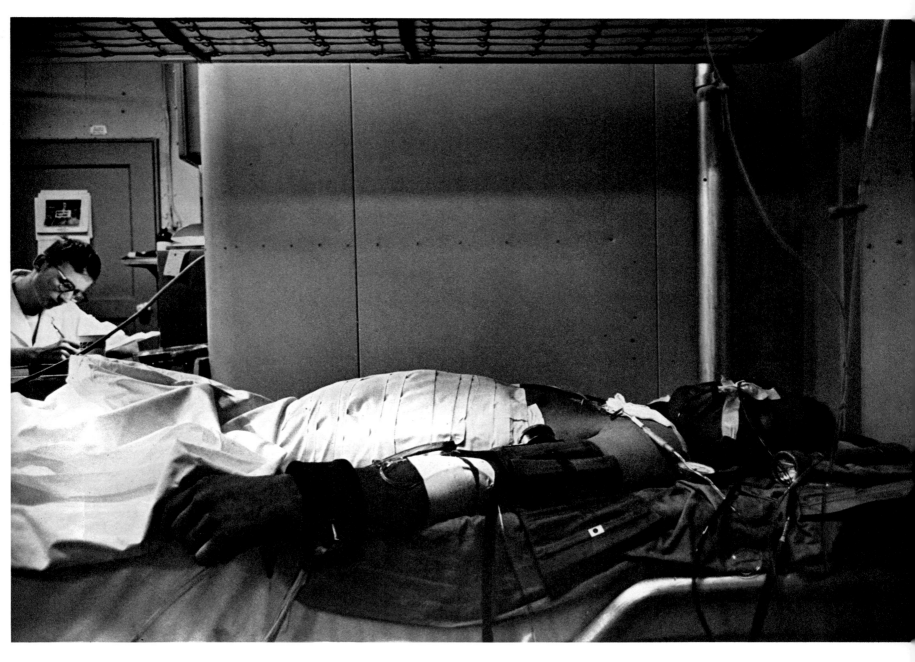

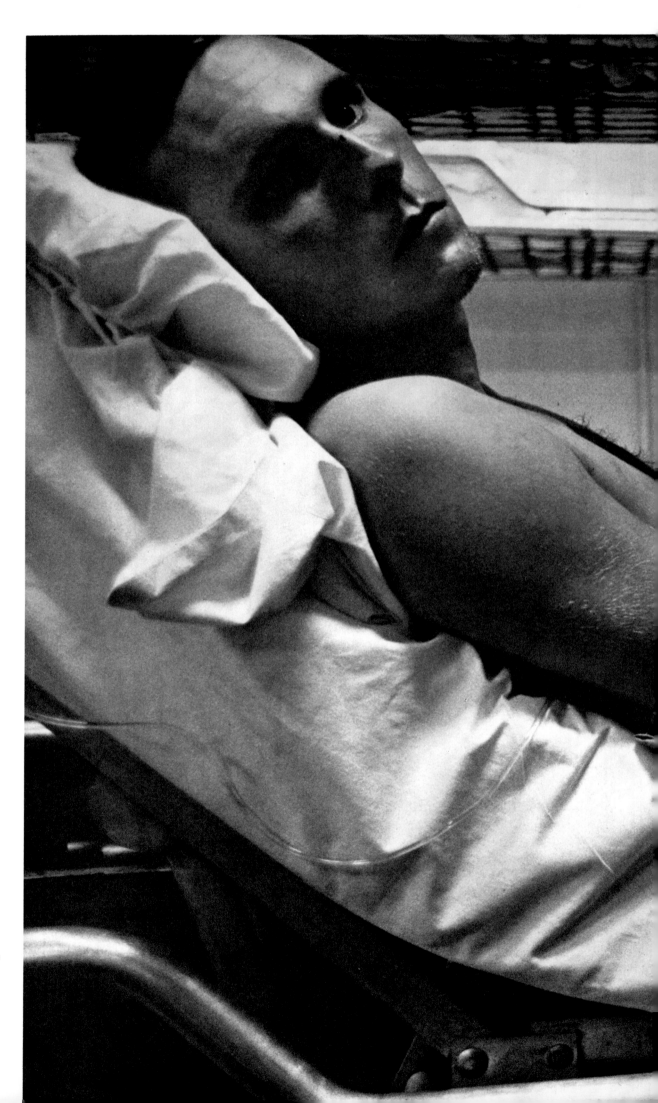

Lance Corporal Doyle Bell;
19; one year in the Marines;
veteran of fourteen attack
missions in six months with
his battalion; radioman for
Captain Reginald Ponsford,
Foxtrot Company commander
who spearheaded the push
from Cua Viet to the DMZ
for Fortress Sentry:

They had boarded a landing
craft at 0300 and headed
for Red Beach on a raging,
storm-blackened sea with
heavy rain cutting visibility
almost to zero. Halfway to
shore—somewhere around a
thousand yards out among the
whitecaps—a giant wave
smashed against their bow and
Corporal Bell fell overboard,
weighted with rifle, ammo
and his heavy radio pack.
Captain Ponsford ripped off
his own gear and dived from
the stern. Reversing his
engines, the pilot had tried
to keep the Captain in sight,
but he was instantly lost.

Captain Ponsford swam back
and down, somehow found
Bell, locked a hand on the
top of his head and dragged
him to the surface, where,
by chance, both were then
picked up in the spotlights
of the landing craft. Once
ashore, Bell was rushed to
the *Tripoli*, nearly dead.
Captain Ponsford went on
to lead his original mission,
with only chapped and salt-
blistered hands revealing
his predawn swim.

Recovering consciousness,
before learning who saved him,
Corporal Bell whispered one
request of the doctor:
"Sir, may I ask a question...
did they find my radio?"

56

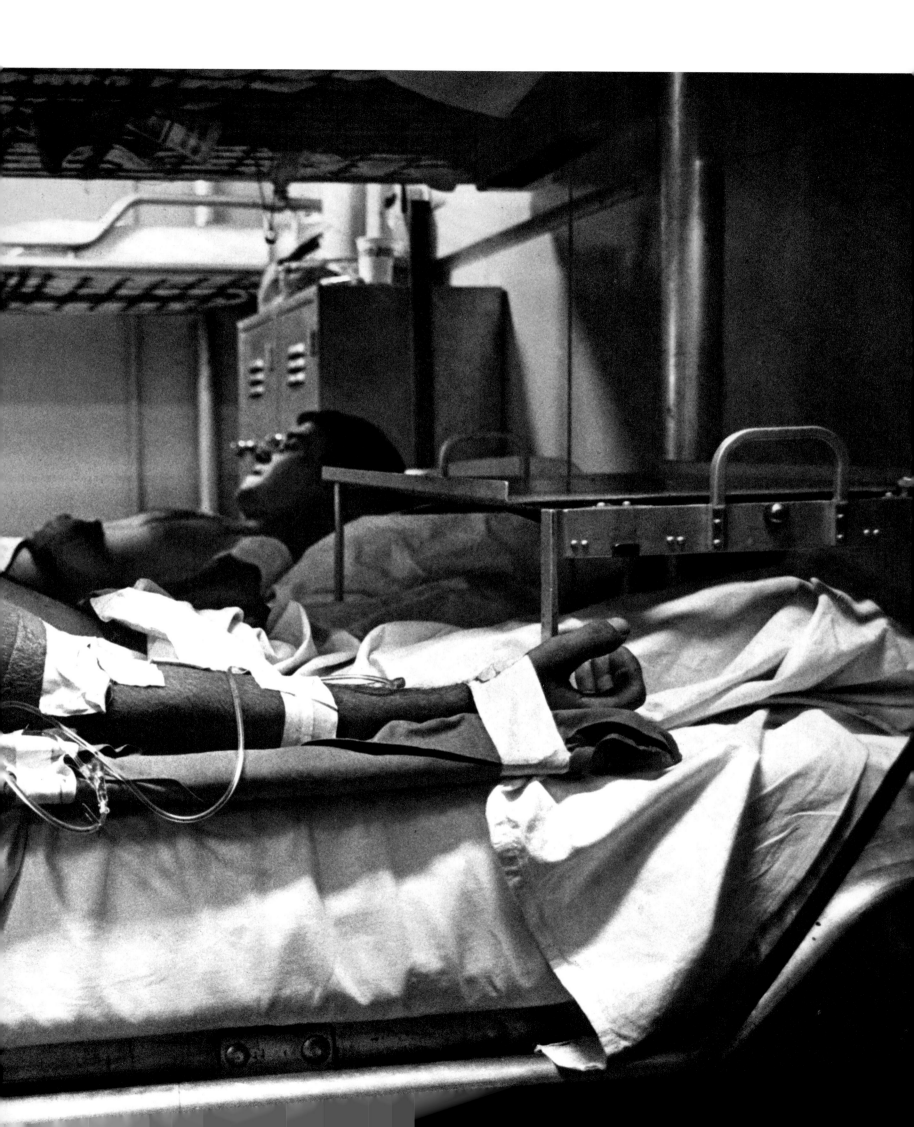

"This is all a dream. It can't be real. Not even you grunts—
nothing here is real!" *Voice at night in Mike Company bunker*

"Sure wish I had this bunker Stateside... *Blissful Bunker
Bar-B-Q*... water running in one end 'n' out the other. I'd sure
have it made! 'Course, Health 'n' Food fellers would never
gimme a license." *Sgt. Charles Sistek, 106-mm recoilless rifle
section, Mike Company*

"Anybody who *is* anybody can get shot—five hundred Marines
on this hill cain't be wrong." *Voice in bunker, late at night*

"I've just found my philosophy for this hill: a philosophy of
nonconsciousness. I don't think about the rounds coming in.
I go wherever I wish. But—I do look for the nearest good hole,
subconsciously." *Lt. Joe Williams, before being shot by sniper*

"Of course, for the shell that hits you, you're in the direct
line of flight—there really is no warning whoosh at all.
You're hit. And that's that." *Old-timer reassuring newcomer*

"Hang down your head Uncle Ho,
Hang down your head and cry.
Hang down your head Uncle Ho,
Poor Boy your men are gonna die.

"They sent us up the mountain,
We had to fight or die.
Five hundred gooks killed there,
and Uncle Ho began to cry." *Ballad of Pfc. Edward C. Miller*

"Good evening, Charles. Yes, Charles, we know you're there.
Charles and us—a real sin-phoney! A fiddle duel, like up at
Corn-eggy Hall in Nooo York." *Lt. Kermit Brown, commanding
Mike Company's attached 106-mm recoilless rifle section, as
Marines and North Vietnamese gunners exchanged night fire*

"... and those Pan Am stewardesses back in Miami, being taught
grace and manners—and judo!" *Noises of rations being opened*

"Charles ain't seen nobody like us! We're so fouled-up we
know not what we're doin' and never do it the same way twice.
Charles may as well quit... he'll never beat us!" *Lt. Brown*

"Real groovy!" *Sgt. Charles Sistek, B-52 bombers having
blasted enemy positions out in DMZ, making Mike Company
bunker tremble*

September–October

1967
Con Thien

Once, in peacetime—nearly thirty years earlier—the cratered knoll rising only about five hundred feet above the gently undulating DMZ countryside to the north had been known to local missionairies as "The Hill of Angels"...Con Thien. Farther north and to the west the land slanted steeply to become the saw-toothed trackless mountain peaks of North Viet-Nam and Laos. Yet it was those few hundred feet of red-clay elevation—lifting it that much closer to heaven in missionary eyes—which gave the hillock a special tactical value to the entrenched commanders facing each other across the DMZ. Con Thien was the greatest natural observation post along the entire battleline between South and North Viet-Nam.

From the heights of Con Thien, the men of Mike Company, 3rd Battalion, 9th Regiment, 3rd Marine Division, looked down upon the DMZ during daily fighter-bomber attacks—and, at the same time, they often saw muzzle flashes of enemy guns when they seared the hilltop with return fire. Saigon and Hanoi considered the place priceless. Mike Company Marines viewed it through rather different eyes.

"I'll bet the first time a gook was shot with an M-16, bet they wondered what the hell hit him—in his belly, up through his gizzard, poked around his teeth, down through his heart 'n' dingus and out his bunghole." *Night voice on far side of bunker*

"The Vietnam war is 'a hell hole of racism for the Negroes GIs over and above the usual hell of war. (Philadelphia *Independent*)' Your real enemies are those who call you 'Niggers.' Your genuine struggle is on your native land. GO HOME NOW AND ALIVE" *Vietcong bomb-leaflet*

"Don't you like shavin'...isn't it a lot of f-----'fun! Every other day, too." "You heard orders—shave today!" "I don't have to...ain't nothin' to shave." *Voices from trench*

"Away from home, away from home; I'm so sad and all alone 'cause now I'm ten thousand miles away from home.

"Here I'm all alone on this hill so far from home. Here I'll fight and make my stand at Con Thien.

"Now we'll fight if we must, but we never fight just for lust; to save the people's land is enough, at Con Thien.

"And the Marines who fought and died for Viet-Nam's *precious* pride; don't forget the blood they shed at Con Thien.

"Away from home, away from home; I'm so sad and all alone, 'cause now I'm ten thousand miles away from home." *Ballad of Corporal Harold Harrington*

Back at the landing zone in the rear—as though there were any rear at Con Thien—each day's incoming traffic of replacements and supplies flowed past the outgoing traffic from the hill; traffic which revealed the true nature of the battleground even on one of those quiet days when the LZ-men could try drying themselves in the open. No rockets or mortars had fallen on them for an hour—the LZ apparently being ground zero on the North Vietnamese artillery maps. And as the LZ-men talked and sunbathed, they were oblivious to all friendly ordinary sounds—like the air strike at the edge of their perimeter, which made the whistling shroosh of incoming rockets difficult to hear. A sound never again to rip across the lives of those other 3rd Battalion Marines now sealed in opaque plastic bags, waiting to be flown home.

Giant helicopters made the run to Con Thien, hauling vast netloads of ammunition, rations, drinking water, medical supplies and sometimes cold milk, fresh fruit and even real ice cream from the supporting base at Dong Ha, on the outside. The chopper pilots hovered ever lower, to drop for an instant—so those men in their silver cocoons could be rushed aboard—then they were gone just as they had arrived, flying barely above the earth trying to evade detection by observers for gunners north of the DMZ.

The helicopter with their dead comrades had been gone only moments
when, from an empty sky, the LZ-men and nearby tank crews found
themselves again under a deadly firestorm of exploding enemy shells.
North Vietnamese artillerymen had them boresighted with 152-mm
guns hidden in well-camouflaged caves ten miles north of the DMZ.
The hillcrest of Con Thien was the most conspicuous promontory
along the entire frontier: even bumbling gunners could hardly miss it.

A first salvo of three shells hit one hundred meters beyond the
LZ-men, who flattened themselves in a slit trench near the tanks.
Sure that a second salvo was already on its way, other Marines
streaked for cover—knowing that no sound would give it away:
there never was warning when they came straight at you....

One Marine had dived for a gully, while
five more piled into a bunker—with ammo
all around. Charlie was walking his barrage
right in upon them. The second salvo erupted
in a supply dump fifty meters dead ahead.

No one spoke, no one moved—no other place
to go. It was too late. Salvo number three
was already coming. The men just waited.
They all knew, by then, that the enemy gunner
was shortening his range by fifty meters a salvo.
The helicopter landing zone was Target Zero.

Then eardrums and hearts and dreams burst.

Three shells crashed on the bunker's outer
flank, fifteen feet away—and the men were
alive, deaf, with muddy boots in their faces.
Not deaf! Another salvo echoed far-off,
fifty meters behind the bunker. Beautiful—
until they heard the worst sound of all.

From Target Zero minus fifty…"Corpsman!"

72

Corpsmen came. A bunker at Target Zero minus fifty
had been hit. Litter bearers converged from everywhere,
gathering around fallen men—a timeless battle requiem.
They carried the wounded to the battalion aid station,
three hundred yards away. And it seemed very far....

Their artillery would soon return to rake Con Thien, searching
for anyone who moved and for a medevac chopper trying to land.
The doctor had only a few minutes to stop the hemorrhaging
and to clean away the mud. He worked under flashlights—
an exploding rocket had knocked out the power plant, once again.

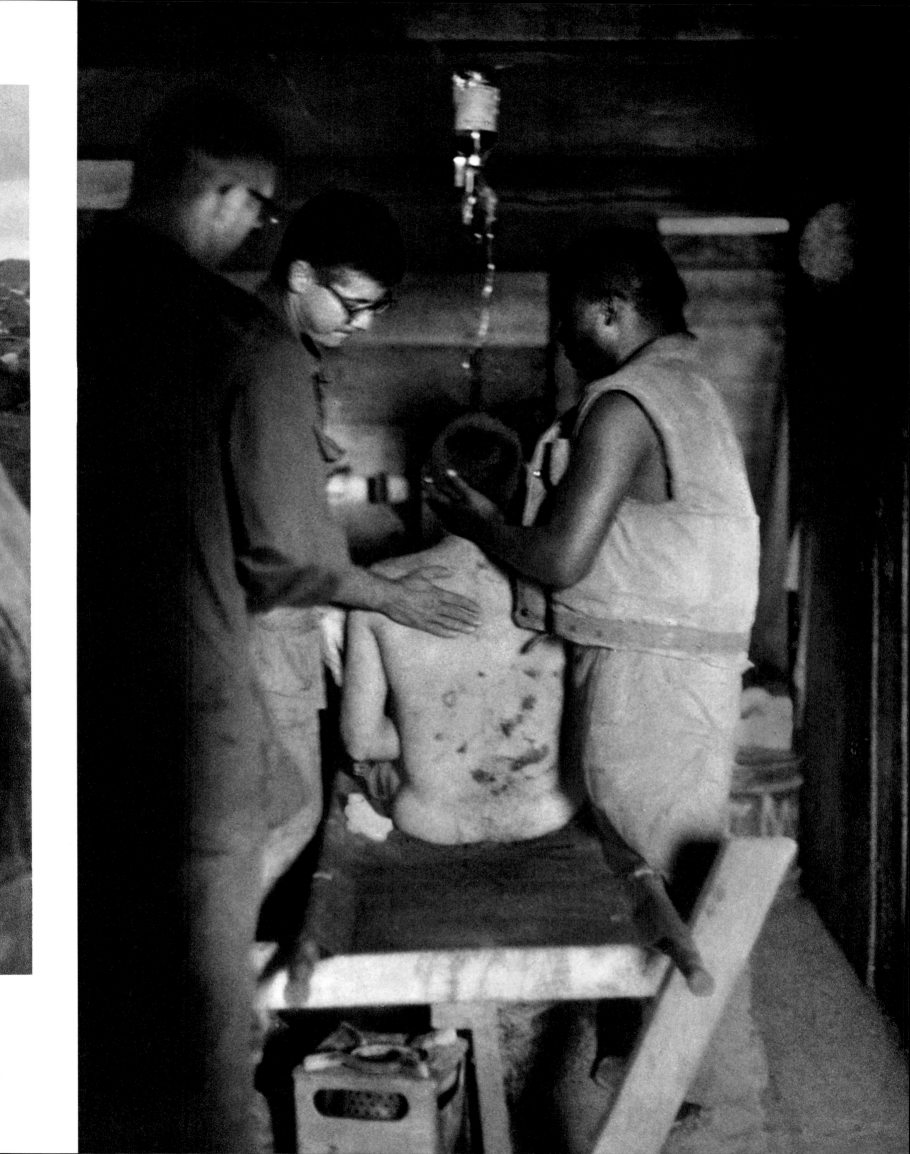

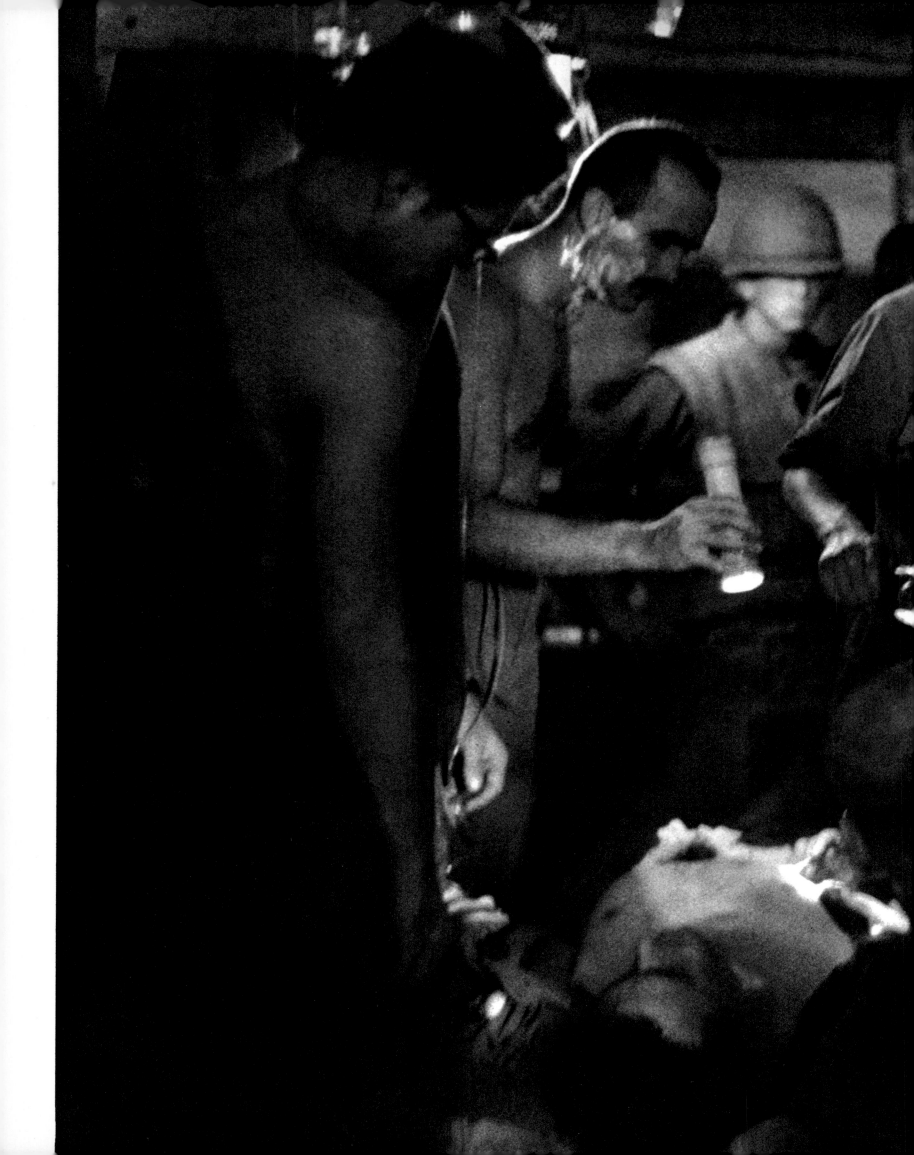

One medevac helicopter wheeled low over the sandbagged aid station but was forced to flee when rockets and heavy mortars drove everyone underground again. The next chopper made it, sweeping even lower, thumping down into the mud. There was a frenzied tender exchange—recoilless rifles for wounded men. Inside, a delirious, suddenly thrashing bomb-stunned Marine was comforted like a child by waist-gunners of abandoned guns. Guns were useless...the plane seemed on the ground forever.

Another wounded man was rushed down from over the treeless hilltop. He arrived at the battered meadow alongside the aid station an instant before the medevac chopper lifted, and then was gone; back to the forward-area main hospital at Dong Ha.

Con Thien settled again into its role of being an eternal sort of place for the Marines burrowed deep in foxholes and tunnels, and reinforced command bunkers under its red-clay mud...a place where calendars were marked not by dates but by monsoon floods, near-misses, another Purple Heart or the death of a friend.

It was a place where a man found that he could sleep relaxed, out in the fresh rain-swept air of a late-autumn afternoon; casually indifferent to streamers of smoke still drifting across the ravine below—smoke that would have come from raked leaves burning back home. Relaxed, despite enemy rockets' having earlier blasted another bunker, setting it afire—relaxed, even though the ravine itself was notorious, sharing with the helicopter landing zone the reputation of being Con Thien's most lethal slice of overdeveloped real estate: "Death Valley."

Beyond the ridge overlooking Death Valley, on the forward slope of Con Thien and facing the DMZ itself, living—and of course dying—was rather informal. In between monsoon rainstorms, when the heat and humidity became too oppressive, the Marines found survival itself almost intolerable within the acrid shell of their own sweat and red dust. So they stripped and waded into the nearest natural bathtub, a rain-filled hollow made by bulldozers when the engineers scooped out Mike Company's command bunker. They stripped, that is, except for helmet, flak jacket and boots, which after a few weeks on that shrapnel-saturated Vietnamese hillside were viewed as perfectly normal parts of every man's body.

When asked why he had cut off all his hair,
Pfc. Mike Morris gave a logical reason:
"The Lieutenant said he thought it would be a good idea."
And that seemed to be answer enough,
while he decided whether to shave—or wait another week.

That cratered knoll, Con Thien—"The Hill of Angels" to the Vietnamese, "The Graveyard" to the Marines— was a place of no special law except mutual support. Men there shared everything. They alone seemed to be proof that the hill's Vietnamese name was the right one.

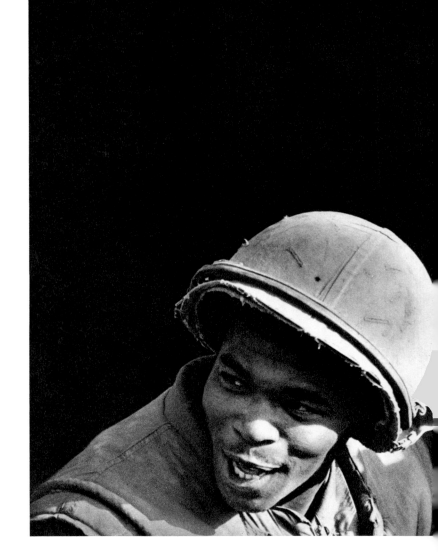

Pfc. Charles Tisby had enlisted in the Marines a year earlier
—the Army was "breathin' down my neck...so why not?"
Tiz, 24, was born in Waskom, Texas, and held a B.S. degree
in biochemistry from Prairie View A. & M. He wanted to own
a pharmacy when he was a civilian again. Tiz's great buddy in
the Con Thien trenches was machine gunner Lance Corporal
Toby Hooten of Fort Smith, Arkansas. He was only 18, but

had been in the Corps three months longer than Tiz and he
towered over his wiry friend. Like everything else, they always
shaved together outside Mike Company's bunker—where
Tiz held off hecklers trying to hurry his usually slower pal.
"Lather up again, Hoot. You missed some first time around."
Then to the heckler: "Man—with his muscles, and my mind,
you gonna tangle with *us?*"

One man was black—one white;
the endless nights and days,
the rain-flooded trench,
constant enemy shelling,
cigarettes, and the grim life
which they shared were the same.

When rain lashed Con Thien, mud and mist enfolded the Marines in a grip from which there was no escape. It would be like that or worse until the next spring, when the monsoons ended. Almost all air support stopped. Only lonely choppers hedgehopped over the primeval misery of the front to bring in emergency supplies and evacuate the wounded. Yet it *was* better when skies turned foul; the enemy's guns flooded out, his ammo bogged down along the supply trails, and, best of all, his prowling forward observers then sat blinded out in the DMZ morass...mute and harmless.

Every Marine journeyed through each night in his own way,
with stops at memories of home, plans for the future and
fantasy after fantasy where every chrome-plated deal worked.
He lived in the sustaining world of a combat infantryman's
imagination, shielded and reassured by the silent presence
of another Marine in the trench beside him, or the next foxhole,
whose dreams were probably interchangeable with his own.

Life was somewhat easier for those men assigned to the command
bunker—radiomen, medics, off-duty crewmen of the recoilless
rifles, the captain and some of his lieutenants—the big brass
of a rifle company. The sandbag-reinforced doorway leading down
into the bunker was special, too, for it gave good light and
almost total security to the grunt who wanted to catch up on
those paperback comics from home—a forlorn, mud-booted man
who recalled the soldier in rotting trenches at Verdun and the
Argonne, or even earlier...in the Civil War.

Candles...muffled men's voices in the gloom
...water gurgling underfoot whenever anyone
moved...an ominous heavy clunk as hand weapon
struck hand weapon...eyes glittering and sweat-
outlined faces catching the candlelight even
where it faded in the overcrowded bunker:
well might Mike Company's grotto have served
those warriors of history's First Crusade; or
others plotting among the catacombs under Rome.

108

By night, their world spun around Mike Company's bunker, overlooking a no-man's-land sporadically lit by flares and tracers and the scorching blast of their recoilless rifles. As soon as Captain Frank Breth had briefed his platoon lieutenants, every man in that massively timbered haven ripped open rations and began cooking, cleaning weapons, writing home or talking: of Communism; of there being no retreat for a Marine; of God— an intensely personal God; of their hatred but respect for enemy Charlie. Then the bunker was silent but for the rhythm of breathing, and the frogs in the monsoon puddles above.

When B-52 bombs fell on the DMZ a mile in front of their lines and Observation Post One, shaking the bunker, a voice came from the darkness: "That's the most beautiful sound on this earth."

"Captain—I've been hit...."
The voice on the field phone
from OP One was perfectly
calm, although the sand-
bagged position—blasted
by a recoilless rifle from
the DMZ—was nearly a ruin.
Corpsmen Dennis McLean
and Bill Dancy had observer
Corporal Harry Hutchinson
back in Mike Company's
bunker almost before shock
set in—but not before he
weakly joked, "Oh, mercy,
friends, whatever was that
noise?" Shock, concussion,
the burned arm and the
sense of humor apparently
balanced each other.
Harry Hutchinson was back
in OP One two nights later.

...survival...letters from home...chow...
the number of days still remaining before a Marine's thirteen-month
combat tour was finished and a grunt waved good-bye to Viet-Nam...
nothing else really mattered—not to those muddy men holding Con Thien.

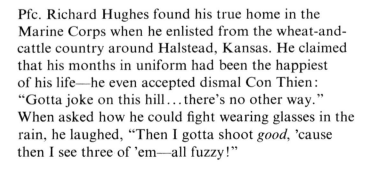

Pfc. Richard Hughes found his true home in the
Marine Corps when he enlisted from the wheat-and-
cattle country around Halstead, Kansas. He claimed
that his months in uniform had been the happiest
of his life—he even accepted dismal Con Thien:
"Gotta joke on this hill...there's no other way."
When asked how he could fight wearing glasses in the
rain, he laughed, "Then I gotta shoot *good*, 'cause
then I see three of 'em—all fuzzy!"

An enemy mortar bomb exploded within ten feet of
Pfc. Richard Hughes late one afternoon while he sat
cleaning his rifle beside Mike Company's sandbagged
bunker. Another Marine diving into the bunker was
instantly killed. Pfc. Hughes was carried back from
the forward slope as soon as the incoming fire lifted.
His rain-fogged glasses stared straight up into the
heavy monsoon sky—apparently the happiest Marine
at Con Thien was dying, too.

"Dead!...Me?...Hell...I'm starved!—they don't even feed
you in this place!" Pfc. Richard Hughes sat on a litter,
using his plastic spoon to clean mud from his boots.
Mortar fragments had creased the back of his head—
knocking him out—torn through his arm and ripped the
seat from his dungarees leaving only minor wounds.
When the medevac chopper arrived, he snarled with outrage
at the litter bearers, "Scram! I walked in—I'll walk out!"
He limped away from Con Thien, where he had been content.

Somehow, the mud-smeared, often bandaged Marines
on that forlorn hilltop seemed at home, oblivious
to water and wounds, and even ready to laugh.
Perhaps their world within our world was enough
unto itself. During a month that the 3rd Battalion,
9th Marines, held their positions at Con Thien,
twenty-seven men died in action; another five hundred
seventy-seven were wounded. Yet, of the wounded,
only seventy-three were evacuated from Viet-Nam.
The other five hundred and four Marines went back
to their country's war—that day their way of life.

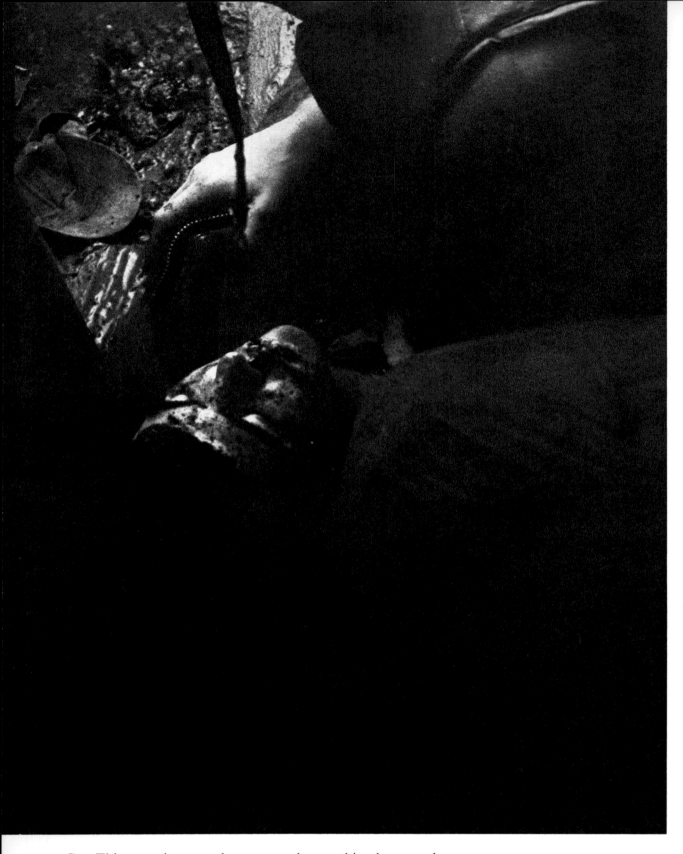

Con Thien was its most dangerous when nothing happened,
when all firing by enemy gunners north of the DMZ had
stopped, and even after their mortar crews just beyond the
Marine lines appeared to be wiped out or slithering away.
During artillery barrages, with everyone underground,
few were hit. But that hilltop was a stalking cobra when quiet.

A single mortar salvo caught the sergeant diving for cover;
Lieutenant Raymos Johnson, sprinting across Death Valley,
was spared. Chaplain Richard Black, never before under fire,
ignored another salvo to come pray for the Marine who fell—
at the bunker entrance where Mike Company always shaved.

After the scramble and dive—rigid, waiting for the shrooshing screech to explode and stop, a man was dead, wounded or once more still alive. And to every Marine on that hilltop the Lord always seemed nearby.

Van Gogh once painted
the bleak beauty of
misery when he lived
with destitute farmers
and miners, telling it
all in grim canvases.
Con Thien reeked with
evil beauty, too, as
darkness fell upon
the trenches and the
monsoon-clouded DMZ,
both silent and waiting.

The Marines prepared
for each night with
loving care—digging
new positions for the
big recoilless rifles;
sneaking "Ontos,"
"The Thing," up into
the firing line at dusk:
multibarreled, deadly.
And riflemen spread a
connoisseur's choice
of grenades, knives and
ammunition nearby—
then settled down to dine.

Dinner finished... weapons handy
... too late to reread the last letter
from home, the Con Thien Marines
started easing into their trenches,
ready for another night among
imaginations and memories, while
waiting for reality from below.

139

...nearly dark.

The birth of
another world
and life—alone.

143

After thirty days
atop Con Thien,
the battalion was
relieved. Not a man
looked back as they
filed off the hill.

The winter monsoons lay upon the land—jungled, mist-enshrouded and shunned by most mountaineer tribesmen, except those who acted as local guides for the North Vietnamese assault divisions which had infiltrated the Marines' area from sanctuary in Laos, six miles west. The Marine "line" which skirted the DMZ was actually a series of self-supporting fire bases sprinkled eastward from the Laotian border to the South China Sea: The Rockpile; Camp Carroll; Cam Lo; Con Thien; Dong Ha; Gio Linh. Ambushes, patrols, choppers and death reigned over the wilderness in between.

During the French-Vietminh war a garrison of Foreign Legionnaires had once based in the same reinforced bunker complex now serving the Marines as a combat operations center. It was abandoned, or overrun, even before the country was split into two Viet-Nams: its past became somewhat murky after the collapse of Dien Bien Phu. Later, no one but a stubborn, romantic French coffee planter saw promise and beauty in the deserted region.

There was no place more remote from Saigon in South Viet-Nam.

Then someone in Saigon, or Washington—or both—poked a finger at the big operations map for the Viet-Nam war and decreed that the Marines should reoccupy the still-intact concrete French command post and its mountain-dominated valley. Arms and supplies were funneling down the Ho Chi Minh Trail from the north, through nearby Laos, into a network of secondary support arteries which converged at the valley before finally fanning out across the Vietcong-saturated frontier zone of South Viet-Nam. The Marines were ordered to interdict the enemy supply routes. Just how the Marines themselves were to be supported in foul weather or during fierce fighting was something else again. As with all such operations, the venture had a code name: Scotland.

"Scotland" soon headlined world news under another name: "The Siege of Khe Sanh."

February

1968

Khe Sanh

Tethered bullocks baiting the enemy tiger...forbidden by Saigon
to patrol beyond their perimeter...six thousand Marines of the
26th Regiment, with three hundred South Vietnamese Rangers
attached, waited behind their sandbags in the fog. They were
under the insistent weight of enemy fire and the threat of
attack by forces greater—probably five times greater—than
their own. General Giap had promised to deliver Khe Sanh to
Hanoi as he had Dien Bien Phu: a Caesar's trophy of war.

The men adapted quickly to showers of rockets and mortars
exploding within their narrow perimeter. It became a life made
richer by the common sharing of everyday events: dividing
equally the can of fruit cocktail in a C-ration; tasting a
few minutes more of life helmet-to-helmet in a slit trench
with a man who had been a stranger before the barrage began,
then suddenly was closer to you than a brother; watching
death roam among you again, accepting His choice without
too deep astonishment that once more you had been spared.

The Khe Sanh Combat Base included a nearby Marine-occupied
hilltop—861 Alpha—part of the screening defenses of Khe Sanh
itself, with its metal-sheathed airstrip. Bullet-torn helicopters
shuttled between the two outposts when fog and incoming fire
were not too dense. On February 5 the enemy launched a predawn
frontal attack against 861 Alpha which left forty-two Marines
crumpled dead or wounded in their trenches and more than
one hundred North Vietnamese soldiers scattered dead at
the barbed wire and around the Marines' foxholes. Another
sector of the Khe Sanh perimeter was breached the morning of
February 8, an attack which before it was crushed took the
lives of twenty-one Marines, with another twenty-six wounded
and three missing. One hundred twenty-four North Vietnamese
died the same morning. Other days were almost as harsh.

With sunrise, if a man lay uncovered upon the ground, he was a
North Vietnamese soldier, just fallen, soon to be buried by
the Marines. If a man on the ground or litter had been
covered with a poncho, he was a Marine killed in action and
awaiting evacuation to the rear, and the journey to his family.
Not much more could be done, in war, for the dead of either side.

The battlefield is a world of final simplicity.

At dawn or dusk, and some days even at noon, fog
cut visibility to less than a feeble hand-grenade
toss at Khe Sanh...and then, other days, bad days,
it fell to zero. The place was hardly ideal as a
base from which to interdict an enemy—any enemy—
with less to qualify it as a defensive position
from which to withstand attacks by the shrewdest
and most experienced guerrilla general in all of
Southeast Asia: Giap, conqueror of Dien Bien Phu.

Many of the Marines assigned to Khe Sanh had been
scarcely in kindergarten in 1954, when Giap scored
his shattering victory over the French Army, and
had heard of Dien Bien Phu only as ancient history
now being updated to apply to themselves and their
stand at Khe Sanh. But regardless of Dien Bien Phu
and Giap and the French defeat, the Marines young
and old in the surrounded outpost had one thing in
common: they recognized a lousy place to fight
when they saw it—and they were now in its center.

Pearly fog...flags from everywhere...graffiti manifestoes on many
helmeted young heads...unlikely objects adorning the barbed wire...
Khe Sanh had a certain charm; and maybe an enemy tunneling underfoot.

Few medevac choppers made a run without being perforated by machine-gun slugs and often returned with wounded—or dead— crewmen. Yet when a call for help crackled at the radio bunker, sleepless pilots hurried to their battered planes, ready to go again.

After 861 Alpha had been hit—hard—in a predawn attack, every plane crew stood alerted, sweating out word from the hilltop that the fog and mortar fire had lifted enough for them to risk landing ammo and evacuating the wounded. The dead could wait.

And their planes had eyes to help them through "Indian Country," which was everywhere. the moment they lifted off the airstrip.

The hilltop lay bare,
sinister, brooding...
shorn of all grace by
the deaths of men who
had just fought there.
The wounded were flown
to Khe Sanh's limited
haven far below.
Sporadic mortar fire
harassed medevacs who
lingered more than
seconds. 861 Alpha
seemed a code name
symbolizing hell,
even as Goya earlier
portrayed hell as
the war ogre—a
monster looming over
the rim of the world.

...hovering choppers
...the soft thrump of distant mortars
...Marines careening around barbed wire into planes
headed for rotation or leave—off the hill, alive
...more ammo and machine-gun barrels and chow and barbed wire
swinging down from the sky
...and the cargo-laden bearers of a tragic safari
hurrying back across the slope with dead friends who
rested on mud-stained ponchos for the last time.

Goya might have felt inspired on 861 Alpha.

With enemy mortars fallen silent,
the wounded and the dead evacuated,
men of Echo Company, 26th Marines,
stood mute in the final debris of battle.
But for their uniforms, it probably
would have looked the same had the
North Vietnamese captured the hill.
Grenades nearby and Bible for solace,
some men who survived slumped alone.

Then everyone went back to work as
Captain Earle Breeding radioed his
report of another night at war.

After blasting the hilltop with mortars, machine-gun fire and grenades,
enemy sappers had breached the Marines' barbed wire with
dynamite-stuffed sections of bamboo. Charging from the night fog,
others leaped sagging wire into foxholes and trenches, where
many of them died fighting hand-to-hand. By dawn the attack
had been shattered and 861 Alpha left a charnel-house shambles.
The fog burned away before noon even in the valley below and the sun
felt good. Marines began repairing their wire; looking much like
farmers pruning their vineyards on the hillsides of Provence—
but for such a different harvest. For then they buried their foe.

The snipers at Khe Sanh worked as three-man teams. After dropping an enemy, each man claimed a kill. Atop 861 Alpha, a team kept the encircling hills swept clear even after the night attackers had been beaten back into more distant concealment; or so they thought.

Two young lance corporals, Albert Miranda and David Burdwell, picked up the enemy soldiers so far away as to be invisible without binoculars or exceptionally keen sight. Miranda kept them in his cross hairs while Burdwell pointed out the targets to their platoon lieutenant, Alec Bodenwiser, the final member of their team. They sometimes sat quietly for hours while stalking with telescopic sights a quarry who, at the fatal instant, probably felt alone—and safe.

Even after his teammates tired and turned away for lunch, sniper Lance Corporal David Burdwell of Wichita Falls, Texas, had remained almost motionless with the rifle. Only his hands moved, and his head, but not his eyes during many long minutes until he shot a far-off enemy soldier...and then he probably looked the same as when he stalked coyotes through the scrublands at home.

On one of those rare sunny days when incoming fire was light
and enemy rocket and artillery observers were snuggled sadly in
their mountainside nests with malfunctioning radios overlooking
naked Khe Sanh; and other North Vietnamese mortarmen were now
out of ammo, having fired most of the night from the deep ravine
north of the perimeter; and a sleepless Marine no longer crouched
in ambush in his trench or bunker or foxhole hoping to murder
another of the lithe jungle rats that infested the place...
on such a special day Khe Sanh was a joy, a casual place where
a trooper shed his helmet and flak jacket and dungaree shirt
and thermal winter-underwear top and settled down—behind flag-
bedecked sandbags, of course—to open a brand-new carton of C-rations
for a midday picnic with his buddy. Other men hurried across
the base for mail call. That same mildew-drying sunshine was
outlining with microscopic clarity every man and piece of equipment
on the airfield in the binoculars of a silent foe above them.

Meanwhile the heart of Khe Sanh throbbed dark and thickly
populated deep underground in the newly refurbished command bunker
built by the Foreign Legionnaires, a useful relic from another war.

189

Day or night, nothing changed for those men in the ancient
Legionnaire bunker except the sense of urgency when Khe Sanh
was under attack. Marines reporting to the combat operations
center dallied in the delicious security of solid-concrete walls
all around and a steel-reinforced ceiling overhead. Air strikes
and artillery barrages were plotted and radioed back to division
headquarters at Dong Ha, unless—as happened so frequently—
attacks built up fast and with ever-greater intensity, at which
time the Khe Sanh controllers went on the air straight to planes
above or to fire directors of the huge 175-mm guns based
at The Rockpile, ten miles to the east. Through it all, veteran
Gunnery Sergeant Leon Risch—six feet five and casual with
that self-assurance of giant men—continued each day with his
floating chess game; pistol, helmet and gas mask at his feet.

In the crowded adjacent bunker—air so dense with old cigarette
smoke as to make even the wall-to-wall operations map swim
before their eyes—the commanding officer of the beleaguered
garrison, Colonel David Lownds, slouched in his ancient canvas
deck chair thickening the smoke with a seemingly eternal cigar.
Throughout the months-long siege numerous crises arose which
the outside world viewed as heralding the fall of the outpost.
Colonel Lownds shrugged with mildly censorious disdain, leaning
back with another cigar and plans to hold Khe Sanh forever.

Days lengthened into weeks into months. Of all the 26th Regiment Marines holding Khe Sanh against General Giap, none was more important than another Asian, wearing an American uniform, in the bunker itself. Bespectacled and scholarly and speaking in Bren-gun bursts, Captain Munir Baig, target intelligence officer, was a renegade Pakistani-Mongol-turned-Marine, son of a lieutenant general of the Indian Army. Colonel Lownds tracked his encircling enemy on Captain Baig's maps; his data from secret devices around Khe Sanh. It was the biggest chess game being played in Viet-Nam, with Giap matched against a master who anticipated his every move.

Captain Baig's closest colleague in the
underground headquarters was intelligence
officer Major Jerry Hudson, who, like the
"Mad Mongol," worked around the clock
and tried to nap beside field phones that
jolted them upright in emergencies, which
were frequent. And because the enemy had
also begun using tear gas during attacks,
Major Hudson kept his mask alongside his
rifle. Knowing that the Vietcong had often
bivouacked in the old French dugout before
the Marines arrived, no one in the bunker
had the slightest doubt about Giap's first
target if his men now overran the place.
Aboveground, when fog, mortars or rockets
closed the runway, Khe Sanh began to die.

Foxholes and trenches always seemed miles away—on the other side of the world—when rocket barrages began crashing upon the Marines at Khe Sanh. Each man counted on two seconds from the first guttural approaching moan until another drab chunk of their perimeter blew apart...hopefully not where he was lying motionless, trying to disappear, too rigid to breathe.

North Vietnamese gunners, controlled by always-moving ridgetop observers, rarely missed hitting something or someone, every salvo. So the Marines lived like prairie dogs, in and out of their vast colony of bunkers. On tough days five or six 122-mm rockets hurtled in every minute. It took a special sort of man to stand quietly during such an attack while guiding other men to cover.

The burrowing Marines also revealed a unique sort of humor in signs left behind while running for their lives.

The hoarse-voiced nine-foot rockets were fired in salvos
of three; a habit so fixed that the Marines waited for the
third to explode—then made their breaks to rush wounded
men to the nearest aid station; or search hastily for better
cover; or wander dazed subconsciously seeking escape;
or race to the edge of the runway for other casualties being
medevacked to the suddenly overburdened doctors...with
the chopper pilots typically flying in through the worst of
the enemy firestorms. Mortar salvos followed the rockets:
one exploded under a just-landed C-130, felling a crewman.

The only words that mattered after a while were "Incoming" and "Outgoing." Rockets, mortars and artillery shells exploding within the perimeter spoke their own gross language. It was very easy to understand. "Outgoing" by comparison seemed almost festive. There was the throaty whine of an artillery round, the reedy whistle of mortars and, most spectacular of all, a close air strike which brought the defenders out of their bunkers.

Marines in Phantom jets strafed, hurled napalm canisters and dropped finned bombs on the enemy sometimes only yards beyond the front trenches. They were sights and sounds so familiar some men scarcely bothered turning their heads when the jets thundered by, bombs erupting just below the runway. Of course, they knew it probably would be their turn as soon as the planes streaked for home.

207

Planes—faster than sound—vanished
behind trees and into nearby ravines,
spewing plumes of noxious black smoke,
their rockets' tails. All attacks upon
Khe Sanh stopped, for the moment.

Of all the thousands of men whose lives were constantly in
danger at Khe Sanh, no one risked them more casually or with
greater frequency than the workhorse crews who barreled the
giant C-130 transports in at treetop to shoot landings on the
metal-slabbed airstrip. Enemy ambushes and monsoon cloudbursts
had cut the only road winding back through the mountains and
rain forest, soon after the 26th Marines were ordered to Khe Sanh.
Unarmed, the massive planes were under machine-gun fire from
the moment they first lowered their wheels and began their
ruler-straight approach. There was no other way: the fortress
had but one runway. North Vietnamese sharpshooters simply
set up their machine guns; waited for the Yank fliers. It
seemed astonishing any planes made it at all. Yet they did,
and they alone kept the Marines at Khe Sanh fed and armed,
and filled with the hope that one day they might be on the
next big beautiful transport headed out, and still alive.

A loaded C-130, machine-gunned during its final seconds in the air, skidded the length of the runway in a fireball of its own cargo—aviation fuel—and exploded, killing one crewman and five passengers. Struggling to reach them—and to clear the runway—rescue teams fought the holocaust with foam. One rescuer had to be saved himself when overcome by smoke.

Rescuers edged their fire trucks directly against
the flaming plane, aiming high-pressure foam
at the inferno's heart. They ignored suffocating
heat and the danger of other fuel tanks bursting
into geysers of burning gasoline. The fire chief,
without even a mask, had tried to enter the cabin,
but its roof collapsed just ahead of him.

It had been hopeless from the start.

Finally, the rescue team chief, never having found time to put on his mask, stood exhausted by the hulk of the plane. And helpless tears streaked his face.

220

When a Marine's hootch—sandbagged foxhole—
took a direct hit from an enemy 122-mm rocket,
rather little usually remained to engross the
casual passers-by of a misty tropical morn.

It was much worse, naturally, when a rocket
landed dead-center in the local ammo dump.
Explosions devastated a nightmare moonscape
among hootches for hundreds of yards around.

The twisted medevac choppers; Pfc. Terry Blanchford of Miami, Florida; Staff Sergeant Loia Paopao of Pago Pago, Samoa; and the still-unexploded artillery shells so tenderly buried, all shared one experience: being in Khe Sanh when the ammo dump blew.

The Gunnery Sergeant, Harrison Relyea, had an ideal job when he came to Khe Sanh— mess sergeant at a base where everyone *loved* everything he put before them. He was soon unemployed, as much as any Marine at Khe Sanh could be unemployed. Rockets had leveled his mess hall. The grunts now were eating most of their meals on the run, or underground.

Sergeant Relyea had fought his way down past Chinese ambushes at the Yalu River, then walked out from Chosin Reservoir through that Korean winter of 1950. Now, he watched quietly through expert eyes, judging fire teams running to the blaze, after rockets hit an aviation fuel dump far up the runway.

One lucky rocketeer had scored,
a direct hit on a cluster of fuel hoses,
turning them into sputtering fuses
leading straight to the gasoline tanks,
side-by-side and filled spigot-high.

Fuel tenders and firemen
with chemical extinguishers
prayed that no unseen spark
would find a fume-filled hose,
to send that end of the airstrip
skyward in one belch of flames.
And as they fought—their lives
finely balanced with their fates—
they created an epic ballet of men, alone.

Wounded at the same moment, in the same places, by the same machine gun shooting through their plane, bandaged airmen awaiting evacuation watched other men far away—a couple of hundred yards—fighting to control the fuel-dump fire.

And they may have wondered about fate and luck—their luck; and the luck of every man at Khe Sanh, like the fire fighters—reflecting on that constant question which accompanied every soldier into combat. How did God choose between them... those permitted to live unwounded... those who died, like the latest helicopter crewmen... and those who though wounded still survived? How? And why me?

Between artillery, rocket and mortar barrages—one day saw over thirteen hundred shells explode on Khe Sanh—the Marines seemed compelled, without hint of shyness, to wonder aloud about their fate...luck or God?

Pfc. Joseph Marshall of Alexandria, Louisiana, 18, knew of no conflict or even question—it had been resolved long before he arrived in that distant valley where he turned to beloved spirituals learned in the church choir at home. And they seemed to help...up to a point.

One night while on sentry duty atop the command bunker in the center of the Khe Sanh Combat Base perimeter and over a hundred yards from the front lines, he was told he could assume that the sudden thrashing and snarled curses in nearby barbed wire came from snagged wandering Marines. Pfc. Joseph Marshall still sighted down the barrel of his M-16. "I'd sure hate to assume wrong."

Lucky cards protected one young Marine...another half-dared fate
each day with his helmet...nearby, a medevac pilot's life depended on
four surgeons—while the gunner and Khe Sanh's senior commander,
Major General Rathvon Tompkins, flew in under fire to the outpost.
There, at dusk, one's luck or fate often seemed to rest in other Hands.

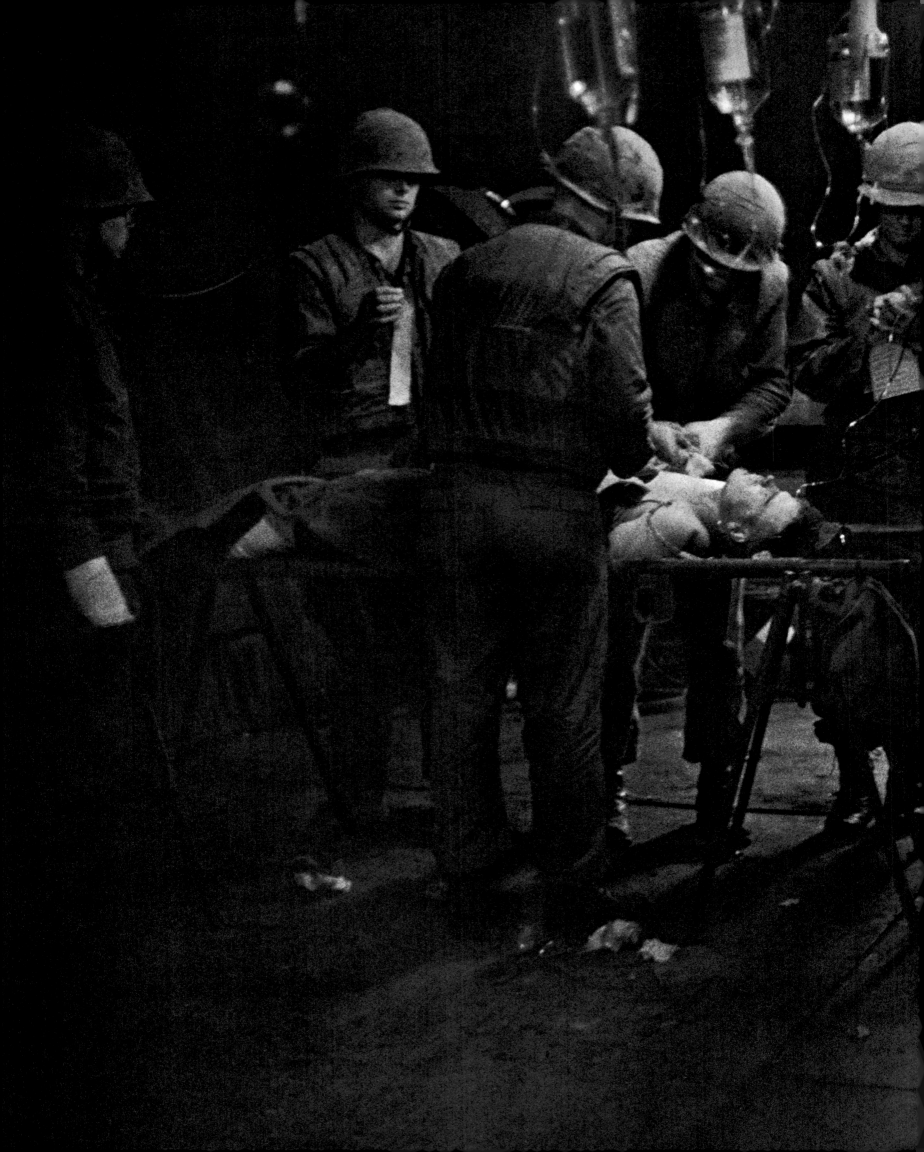

Clouds sank lower upon
Khe Sanh and its airfield.
Clouds dank and drear
and filled with winter chill.
Clouds that fogged and
blinded the eyes of those
enemy rocket and mortar
and artillery spotters
who looked down upon
the besieged garrison;
lonely gunners who had
called their fire with
unvarying precision. So,
the cold, wind-borne clouds
were blessed by the Marines.

Night was near
when two great birds
beat through the clouds
to squat upon the runway—
two gaping-beaked, potbellied
prehistoric birds: messengers
come now to carry off the
fallen men of that day's battle.
Men joining those other men
killed in all other wars.
Then they were gone.

And it was night.